MW00614382

JESUS, BOMBS, & ICE CREAM
STUDY GUIDE

BUiLDiNG A
MORE PEACEFUL
WORLD

JESUS, BOMBS, & ICE CREAM

SHANE CLAIBORNE,
BEN COHEN,
& FRIENDS

ZONDERVAN®

ZONDERVAN.com/
AUTHORTRACKER
follow your favorite authors

ZONDERVAN

Jesus, Bombs, and Ice Cream Study Guide
Copyright © 2012 by The Simple Way

This title is also available as a Zondervan ebook. Visit www.zondervan.com/ebooks.

Requests for information should be addressed to:

Zondervan, *Grand Rapids, Michigan 49530*

ISBN 978-0-310-69368-0

Cover design and illustration: Beth Rhodes (www.bethmade.com)
Interior design: David Conn

Printed in the United States of America

12 13 14 15 16 17 18 19 /DCI/ 20 19 18 17 16 15 14 13 12 11 10 9 8 7 6 5 4 3 2 1

Contents

Note from the Authors

We have been careful to design this project in a way that invites everyone into the conversation. Whether you are a pacifist or a soldier, a Christian or an atheist, a Republican or a Democrat, whether you prefer Ben and Jerry's or Breyers ... okay, that last one may be going too far ... but you get the picture.

This resource (study guide and video sold separately) is not an apologetic for pacifism or nonviolence ... that's more than we can do here.[1] But it *is* meant to engage everyone in conversation. It is a brainstorm—or a dreamstorm—of how we can move the world away from war ... and toward love.

Know that your voice is welcome, and needed. As you talk, make sure you create space for everyone to share, even if you disagree with them. Invite the opinions of folks who are slow to speak—sometimes they have the deepest wisdom. Share from your experiences, and listen to the experience of others.

---

1. To supplement this content, we recommend that you check out the writing of champions of peace such as John Howard Yoder, Michael Nagler, Dorothy Day, Walter Wink, Stanley Hauerwas, and Gandhi, to name a few. We will recommend some other great materials throughout the book and encourage you to let *Jesus, Bombs, and Ice Cream* inspire you to learn from the other prophetic voices for nonviolence.

Introduction

Every morning we wake up to a world that is filled with violence. One news headline after another devastates us with stories of bloodshed.

Another suicide bombing in Baghdad.

Civil war in Syria.

Drones gone rogue in Afghanistan.

A bus explosion in Bulgaria.

A shooting in a Colorado movie theater.

The threat of a nuclear Iran.

It can almost paralyze us—and make us think that violence is a sad reality we have to accept, a normal part of the human experience.

But some of us are just not willing to accept a world of normative violence.

A growing number of people are tired of violence and militarism and war. We are convinced that every life matters. That every human being is made in the image of God and endowed with immeasurable value. Every time a life is lost, our hearts should break—no matter whether that life is lost in Gaza or in Jerusalem, in New York City or in Baghdad, in Kabul or in Colorado.

We are not willing to accept the world as it is, but insist on building the kind of world we all dream of, the kind of world we know God dreams of.

That's what *Jesus, Bombs, and Ice Cream* is all about. Imagining a world where there are fewer bombs and much more ice cream ... and then creating it!

So join us as you dream new dreams for the world. Grab a few friends who will remind you that you are not crazy ... or who will at least remind you that you are not alone. Don't be afraid to disagree. But make sure you disagree well. Remember, as important as it is to be right, it's just as important to be nice.

And grab some Ben and Jerry's Ice Cream — deep, heavy conversation always goes down a little smoother with a tasty treat.

Let the dreams begin.

We Have a Dream

Session 1

Welcome (5 minutes)

Welcome to session one of *Jesus, Bombs, and Ice Cream*. If this is your first time together as a group, briefly introduce yourselves to each other before you begin.

Introduction (3 minutes)

A verse from the Gospels. "I have come to bring peace, but not like the world brings peace."[1]

And another. "Jesus wept over Jerusalem because it did not know the things that would make for peace."[2]

In Genesis, the first book of the Bible, one of the earliest human interactions outside the Garden of Eden is murder. Cain killed his brother Abel, and we've been killing each other ever since. No doubt Jesus is still weeping over our cities, and over our world.

Many passages in Scripture show tremendous violence, even violence that it appears God sanctions or ordains. There are texts some theologians call "texts of terror," such as Judges 19, where a woman is cut into pieces and her body parts are sent out to the twelve tribes of Israel. The Bible is not foreign to our world of violence — in fact, it is downright eerie how little has changed in a few thousand years. Nonetheless, one of the reasons we have

---

1. Paraphrase of John 14:27: "Peace I leave with you; my peace I give you. I do not give to you as the world gives."

2. Paraphrase of Luke 19:41–42: "As he approached Jerusalem and saw the city, he wept over it and said, 'If you, even you, had only known on this day what would bring you peace — but now it is hidden from your eyes.'"

called this project *Jesus, Bombs, and Ice Cream* is because Jesus offers an unmistakable and captivating critique of violence.

Ron Sider, an influential voice for Christ-based nonviolence, gave a speech at the Mennonite World Conference in 1984 that was catalytic in starting what has become Christian Peacemaker Teams, an ambitious worldwide movement of nonviolent activists committed to "getting in the way" of violence. Hear his words:

> Unless we are prepared to risk injury and death in nonviolent opposition to the injustice our societies foster, we don't dare even whisper another word about pacifism to our sisters and brothers in those desperate lands. Unless we are ready to die developing new nonviolent attempts to reduce international conflict, we should confess that we never really meant the cross was an alternative to the sword. Unless the majority of our people in nuclear nations are ready as congregations to risk social disapproval and government harassment in a clear call to live without nuclear weapons, we should sadly acknowledge that we have betrayed our peacemaking heritage. Making peace is as costly as waging war. Unless we are prepared to pay the cost of peacemaking, we have no right to claim the label or preach the message.[3]

Jesus shows us what love looks like with skin on. "Greater love has no one than this: to lay down one's life"[4] for another. That's where we got this idea that we are to love someone "to death" — even our enemies.

Love looks into the eyes of those who want to hurt us and cries out: "Father, forgive them, for they do not know what they are doing."[5] That's what God is like. On the cross, we see love stare

---

3. The complete text of Ron Sider's presentation on July 28, 1984 at the Mennonite World Conference in Strasbourg, France, entitled "God's People Reconciling" (based on 1 Peter 3:8–12), is available at www.cpt.org/es/resources/writings/sider.

4. John 15:13.

5. Luke 23:34.

evil in the face and offer a dazzling alternative to the sword. It has been said that the problem is not that we have tried the cross and it failed us ... the problem is we haven't tried the cross. After all, who wants to die? But that is precisely the call of Jesus. Love does not kill. Love dies.

In the bromance between Ben and Shane, they didn't agree on every theological or political issue, but they did agree that we need a world with fewer bombs and more ice cream ... and they also agreed that Jesus offers a stunning spiritual example of an alternative to violence.

Video Teaching (14 minutes)

As you watch the session one video segment, use the following outline to take notes on anything that stands out to you.

Notes

All is not well in the world.

Our country spends over $30 billion a year on our nuclear arsenal.

Here is some great news: the US's most powerful bomb—the B53—is being dismantled! This bomb is 600 times the size of the Hiroshima bomb that killed 140,000 people.

The epidemic of violence

Michael Rosario's poem

> So just think about the world as a better place
> As we all sit here expressing faith.
> Less bombs, more ice cream.
> Yeah, I said it. More ice cream.
> God bless.

Video Discussion (38 minutes)

1. How are stories of violence, war, and its aftermath part of your history? Do you have any burdens of violence weighing on your life today?

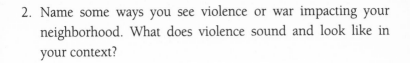

2. Name some ways you see violence or war impacting your neighborhood. What does violence sound and look like in your context?

3. In what ways do you feel you might personally contribute to violence in our world?

4. Read John 14:27. Compare and contrast the kind of peace that Jesus gives with the kind of peace that the world gives. Which do you typically desire more, and why?

5. We often talk of the "dream of peace" in very general ways. Identify three concrete ways you can respond peacefully to the violence in your world. What changes can you initiate by yourself? Which changes might you imagine initiating with a small group, and who would that group be?

Actions to Consider Between Sessions

- Walk through your home, workplace, or neighborhood and identify any objects that are symbols of violence. If appropriate, remove them yourself; otherwise, ask those in charge if they would consider doing so.

- To interrupt the patterns of violence this week, offer peace to one person in your life with whom you may be in conflict.

- Use your creative talents to envision a peaceful world: write, draw, photograph, sing, dance. Share your vision with the group the next time you meet together.

- Read Ron Sider's full address from the 1984 Mennonite World Conference (see footnote 3 for source information). Consider what it really means to be a peacemaker.

- Browse the Sustainable Defense Task Force's website (www. comw.org/pda/usdefpolicy). Choose and read one publication and discuss it the next time you meet.

Helpful Resources

Recommended books, periodicals, websites, movies, and music:

Shane Claiborne and Chris Haw, *Jesus for President* book and tour DVD (Zondervan)

Stanley Hauerwas, *The Peaceable Kingdom: A Primer on Christian Ethics* (University of Notre Dame Press)

Ron Sider, "God's People Reconciling," Mennonite World Conference address, Strasbourg, France, 1984

U2, their 1984 song "The Unforgettable Fire" (preferably with a pint of Dublin Mudslide from Ben and Jerry's)

Winslow T. Wheeler, author and editor, *The Pentagon Labyrinth: 10 Short Essays to Help You Through It* (Center for Defense Information)

Jonathan Wilson-Hartgrove, *The Awakening of Hope* book and DVD study, especially Chapter 7/Session 5, "Why We Would Rather Die Than Kill" (Zondervan)

John Howard Yoder, *The Politics of Jesus* (Wm. B. Eerdmans)

Personal Reflections

Use this space to jot down a prayer or any thoughts and questions this material has sparked. How is God speaking to you?

Our Grief Is Not a Cry for War

Session 2

Checking In (5 minutes)

Before launching into session two's topic, take a few minutes to check in with each other about any of your between-session experiences or other questions or insights you would like to share.

Introduction (3 minutes)

Forgiveness is one of the most powerful forces in the universe. You may remember the shooting incident back in 2006 when a deranged armed man entered an Amish school in Pennsylvania, shot ten children, killing five, and then killed himself.

But do you remember how the victimized community responded?

One of the first things the people did was visit the shooter's family to make sure they were cared for. Next, as they began to receive donations from around the world, the Amish took the generous gifts sent to them and created a scholarship fund ... for the children of the shooter. Finally, the Amish community went to the funerals for their own kids, but then they also attended the funeral for the shooter, so they could be with his family and lament the loss. They grieved together. It caught the whole world's attention.

It makes you wonder what the world would look like if we had had that kind of imagination after September 11.

Redemptive stories of grace, forgiveness, and reconciliation are happening all over the globe, but they don't always make the headlines like the horror stories do. There are victims of violence working for restorative justice rather than punitive justice for those who committed violence. Catholics and Protestants are living together in Northern Ireland even though their parents killed each other in the conflicts. Communities in the US are living Dr. King's dream that one day the children of slave owners and the children of slaves would live together as brothers and sisters on the same plot of land. Victims of genocide have adopted the orphaned children whose parents committed the atrocities. Murder victims' families argue against the death penalty for the offenders and have even become surrogate parents for penitent offenders who want to find a new way forward.

Courageous stories hold much more promise for a better world than the banner that hung on Philadelphia's city hall the week after 9/11 which read, "Kill them all and let God sort them out."

After the terrible attacks on September 11, 2001, a pretty remarkable group emerged from the rubble. It began as a support group for family members who lost their most intimate loved ones—those who lost mothers, fathers, husbands, wives, children, sisters, and brothers. In the beginning they got together to grieve, to support each other, to walk through their pain. But as war erupted, with the probabilities of more death and bloodshed rising, these friends and family members banded together to become one of the most compelling and credible voices against the war. Many traveled on delegations to Iraq and Afghanistan as peacemakers and reconcilers, convinced that there had to be another way forward; humanizing rather than killing the "other." They came back with powerful stories of Iraqi and Afghan families giving them gifts to bring home, along with their deepest love and condolences, to the other victims of 9/11.

Their motto became: "Our grief is not a cry for war." Let this motto drown out the drums of war as these courageous folks model the way of radical forgiveness.

Video Teaching (15 minutes)

As you watch the session two video segment, use the following outline to take notes on anything that stands out to you.

Notes

There was so much ugliness after September 11.

"Wars are poor chisels for carving out peaceful tomorrows."
—Dr. Martin Luther King Jr.

September 11 Families for Peaceful Tomorrows was organized by a small group of family members who met in November of 2001 and proclaimed, "Our grief is not a cry for war."

La'Onf—which means *no violence* in Arabic—is fully committed to nonviolence and deeply engaged in working to reclaim civil society in Iraq.

America *must*, must oppose the rising tide of Islamophobia, which is consuming our land. It is just *not* American.

La'Onf proclaimed about their own nation, "Nonviolence is the solution for reform in Iraq and to make Iraq a civil democracy ... people are *not* our enemies, it is *injustice* that we oppose."

Video Discussion (37 minutes)

1. Where were you on September 11, 2001? Talk about that day. In the following weeks and months, how did you see others respond in ways that inspired or disturbed you?

2. When is the last time you wanted to take revenge on someone? How did you negotiate your feelings of anger in that situation?

3. "The US media painted a picture of Iraqis as either violent ter-
    rorists or helpless victims. These members of La'Onf were nei-
    ther. They were fully committed to nonviolence and deeply
    engaged in working to reclaim civil society in their nation"
    [Terry Rockefeller]. What role do stereotypes play in building
    up our fear of other people?

4. The families of the victims of 9/11 went to Iraq to share love
    and grace. Where are some forsaken places or people you
    might visit to be a graceful witness?

5. If, to quote Martin Luther King Jr., "Wars are poor chisels for
    carving out peaceful tomorrows," what are some "good chis-
    els," things you see that can move the world away from vio-
    lence (and toward ice cream)?

6. Read 2 Corinthians 5:14–21. What might being "Christ's am-
    bassadors" committed to "the ministry of reconciliation" look
    like in the practice of your everyday life?

Actions to Consider Between Sessions

- Find time to engage with someone of whom you have a stereotyped view — it might be a homeless person, someone of a different race, someone doing a particular job, or a person of another religion. If possible, consider inviting this person over for dessert. (Perhaps a pint of Ben and Jerry's Imagine Whirled Peace would be particularly fitting!)

- "Redemptive stories of grace, forgiveness, and reconciliation are happening all over the globe, but they don't always make the headlines like the horror stories do." Make it your aim this next week to find one positive story of life, redemption, or heroism every day. Be ready to share one such experience with the group the next time you meet.

- Write a letter to someone you need to forgive. Or perhaps ask for forgiveness from someone you have wronged and deliver it in person.

- *Extra credit option:* Martin Luther King Jr. had one of the preeminent voices for peace in his time and his voice is still relevant today. Read the full text of the sermon entitled "Why I Am Opposed to the War in Vietnam" delivered at the Ebenezer Baptist Church in Atlanta on April 30, 1967. Read it aloud.

Helpful Resources

Recommended books, periodicals, websites, movies, and music:

Control Room documentary film (www.imdb.com/title/tt0391024/)

La'Onf (www.forusa/laonf-making-iraqi-nonviolence-movement)

The Psalters, Christian band (www.psalters.com)

September 11 Families for Peaceful Tomorrows (www.peaceful tomorrows.org/)

Explore these stories of radical forgiveness:

Elias Chacour with David Hazard, *Blood Brothers* (Chosen Books)

Elisabeth Elliot, *Through Gates of Splendor* (Hendrickson Classic Biographies)

Victor Hugo, *Les Miserables* (various publishers or see the film)

Emmanuel Katongole, *Mirror to the Church* (Zondervan)

Donald B. Kraybill, Steven M. Nolt, and David L. Weaver-Zercher, *Amish Grace* (Jossey-Bass)

Jerry Mitchell, "The Preacher and the Klansman" (*Clarion-Ledger*, Jackson, Mississippi)

Desmond Tutu, *No Future Without Forgiveness* (Image)

Personal Reflections

Use this space to jot down a prayer or any thoughts and questions this material has sparked. How is God speaking to you?

_____

_____

_____

_____

_____

_____

_____

_____

_____

_____

_____

_____

_____

Peace Is the Cross We Carry

Session 3

Checking In (5 minutes)

Before launching into session three's topic, take a few minutes to check in with each other about any of your between-session experiences or other questions or insights you would like to share.

Introduction (3 minutes)

Martin Luther King Jr. was one of those prophetic voices who insisted we must challenge the violence of the ghettoes—and the schools and the theaters—and we must challenge the violence of our government.

A US veteran once said, "The biggest lie I have ever been told is that violence is evil, except in war." He went on, "My government told me that. My church told me that. My family told me that … I came back from war and told them the truth—'Violence is not evil, except in war … violence is evil—period.'"

Our kids are getting mixed messages. A few years ago there was a national news story about a second grader in Rhode Island who wore a baseball cap to school that depicted soldiers carrying guns on the front. The school authorities ruled that his hat violated dress code, which did not allow for weapons on clothing—a code established with the kids' best interest in mind, for their safety and protection. But then school authorities pushed for an exception, working to allow for clothing that depicted soldiers with guns, in the interest of promoting "patriotism and democracy."

No wonder our kids are confused. We are too!

People are speaking out of both sides of their mouths. Maybe for those who believe violence is a *necessary evil* in our world, there ought to be a renewed commitment to still call it *evil*.

We must not forget that Timothy McVeigh, who committed the worst act of domestic terror in US history, said that he learned to kill in the first Gulf War. He said engaging in military combat turned him into an "animal." He came back from war mentally deranged and equipped to kill. And then the government that trained him to kill killed him to show the rest of us that it is wrong to kill. There is something deeply troubling about our flawed logic of redemptive violence.

Jesus and other great folks throughout history have challenged the notion that violence can get rid of violence, or that violence can ever be redemptive. They've insisted that it's like fighting fire with fire. Others have argued that violence may be justifiable at times, but it is always evil or sinful, so we should take special care to never call it noble or honorable. Charlie Liteky, one of the guys with whom Shane went to Iraq, is among America's most decorated Vietnam vets and has become one of the most vocal objectors to war. On his peacekeeping mission to Iraq, he often held up a sign that said, "I hate war, as only a veteran can."

We can take courage that Jesus understood the violence of our world very well. He wept over Jerusalem and no doubt he is still weeping over incidents of violence today. And lots of us are weeping with him. Perhaps it's time for a united, nonviolent assault on the myth of redemptive violence. Perhaps it's time for us to declare that violence is always evil—period.

Video Teaching (11 minutes)

As you watch the session three video segment, use the following outline to take notes on anything that stands out to you.

Notes

Logan Mehl-Laituri, a young veteran of the Iraq war, has begun to question our patterns of war.

Service members are falling *on* their swords in greater numbers than are falling *to* the sword. In July, there were more active-duty suicides than there were days in the month.

St. Martin of Tours

In the church, when our heavenly Commander replaces our earthly ones, we call it baptism; it's a time of rebirth in which Peter in the book of Acts reminds us that we pledge a new allegiance to obey God rather than men.

Following the path of enemy love in a world of enemy fear never goes over well.

War has been conquered; it is over, if we want it . . .

Video Discussion (41 minutes)

1. How did you react when you heard Logan's testimony? Discuss.

2. Do you know any soldiers or veterans? Have you ever asked them to share their story with you?

3. With Martin of Tours in mind, how can you think about the Fourth of July in a different way this year? How might you participate in Martinmas on Veteran's Day this year? (Perhaps a pint of Ben and Jerry's Americone Dream would be a delicious accompaniment!)

4. Read the Sermon on the Mount, found in Matthew 5–7. (Note: If time is an issue, concentrate on chapter 5, verses 9–12, 21–22, and 38–48.) What does this text have to say about violence?

5. Describe a time when you followed Jesus' command in Matthew 5:44 to "love your enemies and pray for those who persecute you." How did the experience change you?

Actions to Consider Between Sessions

- Spread a world map out on a table in front of you and identify how many nations are at war—whether within themselves or with other nations. Pray for peace in these conflicts.

- Invite friends and family over for a home screening of the movie *Soldiers of Conscience* (www.imdb.com/title/tt1217603/). Discuss it together.

- The *Common Prayer: A Liturgy for Ordinary Radicals* shares powerful stories of our stream of saints (like Martin of Tours) in the context of daily prayers. Go on a scavenger hunt through the year to identify other days to mourn our violent history and to celebrate our martyred heroes and she-roes. Check out www.commonprayer.net.

- Learn about the work of Centurion's Guild (www.centurions guild.org/) and the care packages they send to soldiers and veterans who are considering the impact of their faith on their military service.

Helpful Resources

Recommended books, periodicals, websites, movies, and music:

Logan Mehl-Laituri, *Reborn on the Fourth of July* (InterVarsity Press)

Derek Webb, the album *Mockingbird*

Tripp York and Justin Bronson Barringer (editors), *A Faith Not Worth Fighting For* (Cascade Books)

For more information on military suicides:

www.cbsnews.com/8301-500690_162-3498625.html

More films on war that Logan recommends:

The Conscientious Objector

The Fog of War

Ground Truth

This Is Where We Take Our Stand

Why We Fight

Winter Soldier

Personal Reflections

Use this space to jot down a prayer or any thoughts and questions this material has sparked. How is God speaking to you?

_____

_____

_____

_____

_____

_____

_____

_____

_____

_____

_____

_____

Under One Blue Sky

Session 4

Checking In (5 minutes)

Before launching into session four's topic, take a few minutes to check in with each other about any of your between-session experiences or other questions or insights you would like to share.

Introduction (3 minutes)

A verse in the Qur'an speaks of how there is one blue sky that covers us all. It points to the fact that each of us is part of this global yet highly dysfunctional humanity, with a family tree that goes back to Abraham and Sarah (and ultimately to Adam and Eve). And so an incredible group of kids in Afghanistan started the "blue scarf" movement, inviting folks around the world to wear blue scarves as a way of remembering that the same sky covers us, the same sun warms us, and the same stars dazzle us.

One of Shane's favorite memories from Iraq was talking to a Christian bishop there after a mind-blowing service where hundreds of Arab Christians gathered to pray for peace. Shane remarked to the bishop, "I had no idea there were so many Christians in Iraq." And, with a smile, the bishop replied gently, "Yes, son, this is where Christianity started." He went on to remind Shane that the Garden of Eden was right down the street. And Jonah was buried around the corner. The bishop said, "This is the land of your ancestors."

Television can distort how we see people. We end up only seeing certain types of Muslims, or certain types of Christians. Extremists of all stripes have distorted the best of our faith traditions and hijacked the headlines with hatred. We see Muslim extremists blowing up things, and we see Christian extremists burning the Qur'an. These are the ugliest forms of faith ... sick religion. Yet too often we identify the worst in "others" and exaggerate those worst things. While we find the best things about "us" and exaggerate those best things. Eventually, we end up with distorted versions of "us" and "them," neither of which is accurate or honest ... and before long our exaggerations and distortions breed acts of hatred and violence.

But there is another way.

Jesus teaches us to look for the worst things in ourselves and for the best things in others. He teaches us not to judge other people, but to work on getting the log out of our own eye so that we can even see them properly. Before we will see a new world, we will need new eyes. Then we can look into the eyes of others and see the image of God in every person. We can look into the face of the oppressed and see our own face, and we can look into the hands of the oppressors and see our own hands. We can see that there is one God who made us all, and there is one blue sky that covers us.

Jesus redefines what it means to be family, asking, "Who are my mother and my brothers?"[1] He challenges our identities to the core — tribalism, nationalism, etc. — and invites us all to be "born again." This means that we have a family bigger than biology and connected with something deeper than DNA. A love for the people near to us is not a bad thing, but our love can't stop at borders.

South Africans have a word *Ubuntu*. There is not an adequate translation into English, but it means that we exist together ... our survival and our future is connected ... your pain is my pain, your joy is my joy ... I cannot become everything I am meant

---

1. Mark 3:33.

to be without you becoming what you are meant to be. When I dehumanize you, I dehumanize myself. The thought that I exist alone, without you, is a lie. No wonder in Rwanda there are signs painted over the mass graves from the genocide that say: "If you had known me, you would not have killed me." Perhaps killing begins with not knowing the other person. And the beginning of a new way of life is to know those we've been told to call "enemy." To live into Ubuntu.

It's hard to love people we don't know. And it's almost impossible to kill people we love.

Video Teaching (15 minutes)

As you watch the session four video segment, use the following outline to take notes on anything that stands out to you.

Notes

I've been to Iraq twice. I can remember one of the worship services where thousands and thousands of Christians were singing "Amazing Grace" in Arabic. I was so moved that I said to an Iraqi bishop afterward, "Sir, I can't believe that there are so many Christians in Iraq." And he said, "Yes, son, this is where it started."

"You didn't invent Christianity in America, son. You guys just domesticated it. You go back and you tell the Christian church in America, we're praying for them. We're praying for them to recapture their imagination."

A new imagination is stirring across the globe. One little expression of that imagination is Friends Without Borders.

Learning from the stories of people who have suffered deeply from the patterns of violence and who still have the courage to build a world without war

"They will beat their *swords* into *plowshares* and their spears into pruning hooks. Nation will not take up sword against nation, nor will they train for war anymore" (Isaiah 2:4; Micah 4:3, emphasis added).

Video Discussion (37 minutes)

1. Often pain and hope are bound up together. Tell stories of how you have experienced this in your own life.

2. In the video, Shane tells a story of an Iraqi bishop who tells him that Christianity was not invented in America—just do-mesticated. What do you think he meant by "domesticated Christianity"?

3. When have you been told to fear someone that you should not have been told to fear? What were the consequences of that advice?

4. Do we expect to "look into the eyes of others and see the image of God"? When have you seen the image of God in someone you might not have expected to?

5. Read John 3:1–21, Jesus' encounter with Nicodemus. What stands out to you in this passage, particularly as it relates to Shane's comments about humanity's interconnectedness?

Actions to Consider Between Sessions

- At the original *Jesus, Bombs, and Ice Cream* event in 2011 we gave out blue scarves to everyone. We didn't get to include one with this study guide, though we did think about it! Explore the Blue Scarf Movement at www.thebluescarf.org. Fashion a blue scarf and wear it as a symbol of your solidarity with the children in Afghanistan as well as with all people around the world affected by war.

- Learn a song or taste a food or adopt a tradition from a different culture or people.

- We can learn so much from the stories of national imagination in El Salvador and in Liberia. Watch the movies *Return to El Salvador* (www.imdb.com/title/tt1593775/) and *Pray the Devil Back to Hell* (www.imdb.com/title/tt1202203/). How did these nations display imagination instead of domestication?

- Join the next Global Days of Listening call. For more information, visit www.globaldaysoflistening.org/.

- Josh Seitzer turned an AK47 into a gardening tool. Now it's your turn. Refashion a "sword into a plow"—and transform something that has symbolized death into something that symbolizes life.

Helpful Resources

Recommended books, periodicals, websites, movies, and music:

Afghan Youth Peace Volunteers (ourjourneytosmile.com/blog/)

Daniel Berrigan, *The Kings and Their Gods: The Pathology of Power* (Wm. B. Eerdmans)

Walter Brueggemann, *The Prophetic Imagination* (Fortress Press)

John Francis (johnfrancismusic.com)

Friends Without Borders (www.friendswithoutborders.net or www.friendswithoutborders.org)

Voices for Creative Nonviolence (vcnv.org/)

Personal Reflections

Use this space to jot down a prayer or any thoughts and questions this material has sparked. How is God speaking to you?

_____

_____

_____

_____

_____

_____

_____

_____

_____

_____

_____

_____

Jesus Disarmed Us All

Session 5

Checking In (5 minutes)

Before launching into session five's topic, take a few minutes to check in with each other about any of your between-session experiences or other questions or insights you would like to share.

Introduction (3 minutes)

Western evangelical Christianity has not been known for its consistent ethic of life—it has often been more pro-birth than pro-life, opposing abortion but not always opposing death when it comes to capital punishment, gun violence, militarism, and poverty. Some must not have understood that when Jesus said to love our enemies, he probably meant we shouldn't kill them.

Even so, Christianity throughout history has had a powerful critique of violence in all its ugly forms. One of the patriarchs, the third-century African bishop Cyprian, noted the contradictory view of death so prevalent in culture, that calls killing evil in some instances and noble in others: "Murder, considered a crime when people commit it singly, is transformed into a virtue when they do it en masse."

Contemporary thinkers such as René Girard contend that this challenge to violence is inherent to Christlike Christianity, at least in part, because at the center of the Christian faith is a victim of violence—Jesus brutally murdered on the cross. Yet there is a triumph over death as he rises from the dead, a final victory over violence and hatred and sin and all ugly things.

Even in the face of evil that Jesus endured, he consistently challenged the myth of redemptive violence. He looked into the eyes of those killing him and called on God to forgive them. He loved his enemies and taught his disciples to do the same. He said, "You've heard that it was said, 'Eye for eye, and tooth for tooth.' But I tell you, do not resist an evil person" and "You've heard that it was said, 'Love your neighbor and hate your enemy.' But I tell you, love your enemies and pray for those who persecute you."[1] He challenges the prevailing logic of his day, and of ours. He insisted that if we "draw the sword [we] will die by the sword."[2] We've surely learned that lesson all too well.

In fact, not only have we drawn the sword and died by the sword over and over again, but we have made a business of sword-selling, or bomb-selling. Over 150 countries have gotten weapons from companies such as Lockheed Martin. And many of these companies are based here in the US and are even subsidized with federal (taxpayers') money. At times we sell weapons to countries as they fight each other (like the well-known Iran-Contra scandal), directly profiting from war. And then we are surprised when those weapons are turned on us, as in the case of Iraq. A well-known Iraqi politician said, "US politicians know that we have some weapons . . . because they have the receipts from them!"

Imagine if we were selling guns to kids in our neighborhood and then saying, "Don't hurt us, or anyone else." The peace will not last. No wonder Jesus in essence taught, "I have come to bring peace . . . but not the way Rome brings peace."[3]

In the Garden of Gethsemane, when one of his disciples picked up a sword to defend him and cut off a guy's ear, Jesus scolded his own disciple, picked up the ear, and healed the wounded perse-

---

1. Matthew 5:38–39, 43–44.

2. Matthew 26:52.

3. Paraphrase of John 14:27.

cutor. The early Christians said, "When Jesus disarmed Peter, he disarmed all of us." After Peter, Christians wouldn't take up the sword again for hundreds of years! The early Christians saw that Jesus may call us to die, but Jesus never calls us to kill. When we kill someone in order to protect someone else, it may seem like the right thing. It may be courageous. It may be patriotic. It may be selfless and sacrificial. But when we kill, it diverges from what love is like—at least what love looks like in Jesus.

Christian theologians have said Jesus teaches a "third way" to interact with evil. We see a Jesus who abhors both passivity and violence and teaches us a new way forward that is neither submission nor assault, neither fight nor flight. He shows us a way to oppose evil without mirroring it, a way in which oppressors can be resisted without being emulated and neutralized without being destroyed.

There is always a third way.

Most of us want a world free of evil. The mission to rid the world of evil is captivating. Plenty of movies and plenty of politicians have championed that mission. It is a hope that taps into our deepest hunger that good should triumph over evil, and that the bad guys should lose in the end. People cheered when Osama bin Laden was killed. But is it possible that no one is beyond redemption?

Grace is a scandalous idea. The thought that someone who has done terrible things can be redeemed or become a new creation can seem absurd ... but that is one of the core claims of the Christian faith. The Bible is full of messed-up people who became people of God. Consider Saul of Tarsus, a notorious persecutor of the early church who went door-to-door trying to annihilate Christians and oversaw the execution of the first Christian martyr, a man named Stephen. And yet God so radically converted Saul that he changed his name to Paul, who went on to write more books of the Bible than anyone else. If we believe that terrorists are beyond redemption, then we should rip out half the New Testament. It was written by one.

God's grace is big. Sometimes it is bigger than our minds, or our hearts, can conceive. African bishop Desmond Tutu says, "God's grace is big enough to set both the oppressed and the oppressors free." May his words ring true in our lives and in our land.

Video Teaching (8 minutes)

As you watch the session five video segment, use the following outline to take notes on anything that stands out to you.

Notes

But Jesus is saying, "You've heard it said, 'An eye for an eye, a tooth for a tooth,' but I want to show you a better way. Love even those who hurt you." It's this way of imagining that disarms violence without mirroring it. There is a different possibility.

The only one who's left with any right to throw a stone has absolutely no inclination to do so. We can learn from that—the closer we are to God, the less we want to throw stones at other people.

"When Jesus disarmed Peter, he disarmed every one of us." Because if ever there was a case for justifying violence, Peter had a pretty good one. We can see that at the center of Christ's message is this truth: There is something worth dying for, but nothing in the world worth killing for. For Christ we can die, but we cannot kill.

As a Christian, I love the resurrection because it's the promise that love can conquer hatred and that life can conquer death.

Video Discussion (44 minutes)

1. Gandhi and King claim "an eye for an eye leaves the whole world blind." Do you ever think violence is necessary? Do you still think it is evil or sinful even if you deem it necessary?

2. Read Luke's account of Jesus' arrest in the Garden of Gethsemane, Luke 22:47–53. Discuss Jesus' various reactions to violence—both the overt violence of the disciples and those who had come to take him as well as the covert violence of Judas.

3. Do you agree with Shane that nonviolence is core to Jesus' message? Are radical love and violence mutually exclusive?

4. It is entirely reasonable to look at history and argue that violence has worked and violence has failed, and the same goes for nonviolence. What historic events and people inform your moral compass regarding war?

Actions to Consider Between Sessions

- Jesus says, "Let the one who is without sin cast the first stone." What stones of blame are you carrying? Which ones will be most difficult for you to put down? Go outside and gather a handful of small stones. Consider using chalk to write the names of those who have harmed you on the stones. And then wash their names away as a tangible way of practicing forgiveness and a third way.

- "Grace can dull even the sharpest sword." Share some stories of grace in your life that you feel have softened the sharp blade of violence and created a space for peacemaking.

- Watch a video of Martin Luther King Jr.'s Riverside Church speech, delivered April 4, 1967, entitled "Beyond Vietnam:

A Time To Break Silence" (www.youtube.com/watch?feature
=player_embedded&v=OC1Ru2p8OfU).

- Make two lists: one of the *things* you value and the other
  of the *people* you value. Which of these lists informs your
  actions more? How can you realign your choices to be more
  people-valued than thing-valued?

Helpful Resources

Recommended books, periodicals, websites, movies, and music:

Eberhard Arnold, *The Early Christians: In Their Own Words* (Plough Publishing)

Greg Barrett, *The Gospel of Rutba* (Orbis)

Christian Peacemaker Teams (www.cpt.org/)

Conspire magazine, Summer 2012 Issue, "The Way of Nonviolence" (subscribe at www.conspiremag.com)

John Dear, *Lazarus Come Forth* (Orbis)

Martin Luther King Jr., *Why We Can't Wait* (Signet Classics)

David LaMatte and Jenn Hales, *White Flour* children's book (Lower Dryad Music, www.davidlamotte.com/white-flour/)

The Mission film (www.imdb.com/title/tt0091530/)

Oscar Romero, *The Violence of Love* (Orbis)

Miraslov Volf, *Exclusion and Embrace: A Theological Exploration of Identity, Otherness, and Reconciliation* (Abingdon)

Personal Reflections

Use this space to jot down a prayer or any thoughts and questions this material has sparked. How is God speaking to you?

_____

_____

_____

_____

_____

_____

_____

_____

_____

_____

_____

_____

_____

Dessert

Session 6

Checking In (5 minutes)

Before launching into session six's topic, take a few minutes to check in with each other about any of your between-session experiences or other questions or insights you would like to share.

Introduction (3 minutes)

Jesus told a powerful story many of us know as "The Parable of the Good Samaritan." We have occasionally used and abused this story to the point that it has lost much of its original edge, but here's the gist of it:

> A guy is walking down the road from Jerusalem to Jericho when he is attacked by some bandits, stripped naked, beaten unconscious, and left in a ditch to die. A priest strolling down the road passes by on the other side (he must have been late to church). Then a Levite (another devout religious guy) comes down the road, sees the guy in the ditch, and also passes by on the other side (no doubt he also had some important religious business to attend to). Then a Samaritan comes walking down the road. [You can almost hear the snickers in the original crowd of listeners. Samaritans were a despised people — they were only partly Jewish, and they worshiped God differently than the Jews in Israel. Most folks went out of their way to travel around Samaria to avoid them.] But the Samaritan is the hero of the story. He bends down into the ditch and rescues the guy, binds up his wounds, takes him to a nearby inn, and contributes his own money to the man's continued care.

There are a few things worth noting in the story:

1. The people you would expect to do something—don't.
2. The cultural villain becomes the story's hero. And it isn't because of his religion, but because of his compassion.
3. The fact that the man is beaten naked and left unconscious is important, because clothing and language (or accent) would be the two ways to identify the man. The point is unmistakable—no matter the person, he or she is worth saving.
4. The story never would have happened if the Samaritan didn't travel down a troubled road. We go out of our way to avoid troubled roads and neighborhoods, but those are the very places where we need to be, so that we might help those who have been run over.

The story is about an interruption. We love routines, schedules, and predictability. But this story invites us to be interrupted by the suffering of others.

Dr. Martin Luther King Jr. preached a great sermon on the Samaritan story in which he challenged the notion that we just need to lift victims out of the ditch. Dr. King said:

> We are called to play the Good Samaritan on life's roadside ... but one day we must come to see that the whole Jericho road must be transformed so that men and women will not be constantly beaten and robbed. True compassion is more than flinging a coin to a beggar. It comes to see that a system that produces beggars needs to be repaved. We are called to be the Good Samaritan, but after you lift so many people out of the ditch you start to ask, maybe the whole road to Jericho needs to be repaved.[1]

We must continue to lift people out of the ditch. But we also need to reimagine the whole road to Jericho. We must take care of those who are being run over. But we also have to drive a stake in the wheel that is running over them.

1. Martin Luther King Jr., "A Time to Break the Silence." Delivered at the Riverside Church in New York City, April 4, 1967.

Video Teaching (13 minutes)

As you watch the session six video segment, use the following outline to take notes on anything that stands out to you.

Notes

We believe there is something spiritual about imagining a world without violence.

"In the councils of government, we must guard against the acquisition of unwarranted influence, whether sought or unsought, by the military-industrial complex. The potential for the disastrous rise of misplaced power exists and will persist." —Dwight D. Eisenhower

The US military budget spends over $1.2 million a minute.

Ben Cohen's Oreo Chart

"A nation that continues year after year to spend more money on military defense than on programs of social uplift is approaching spiritual death." —Dr. Martin Luther King Jr.

Our invitation is to play our little part in the divine conspiracy to make the world a better place.

For some strange reason, God doesn't want to change the world without us.

Video Discussion (39 minutes)

1. Read Jesus' Parable of the Good Samaritan in Luke 10:25–37. Tell about a time when you have been a Good Samaritan. Tell about a time when you have needed a Good Samaritan.

2. Has there been a time when you haven't stopped to help someone in need? Did you regret it? Conversely, has there been a
   time you have stopped to help someone in need? Did you regret it?

3. "Sometimes we're waiting for God and sometimes God is waiting for us." How has this been true in your life?

4. "I was brought up to believe, 'That's just the way things are'"
   [Ben Cohen]. Yet don't we see daily that boundaries are being
   extended and limits are being broken? Where in history has
   the impossible been made possible? How does this affect your
   faith, in believing despite the evidence?

5. "As we dream of the possibilities, everyone has a role to play"
   (Shane remembered the story of the little kid with his lunch
   and the feeding of the five thousand). What looks insignificant
   in your hands but holds incredible possibility?

6. Did Ben's Oreo demonstration bring you any new insights about the national budget? How would you stack your Oreos? If Jesus had to balance the US budget, what might he cut, and what might he not?

Actions to Consider in the Coming Days

- It's been said that budgets are moral documents, meaning they reflect our deepest core values. Look at the federal budget and rearrange spending as if you were president. Share with a few friends what your priorities are when it comes to federal spending.

- If budgets are moral documents (and since most of us will not be president), take a look at your personal or family budget. Ask how you might be contributing to violence, even unintentionally. How might you use less fuel or more fairly traded products and diminish the suffering of others and of the earth?

- Pray for our country and our world.

- Write a politician. Drop a line to a member of Congress or the president and let them know you would like to see more money spent on things that give life rather than on things that destroy life. Be nice.

- Allow your life, like the man on his way to Jericho, to be interrupted by the suffering of others. Stop and help someone who needs help. Stop and talk to someone who needs a listening ear. Slow down and leave space for interruptions (after all, half of the gospel stories are about Jesus being interrupted by someone's crisis or suffering).

- Get a couple of pints of Ben and Jerry's, meet with a friend, and share a few things you learned in this study. For extra credit, do that with someone who's not a friend. For extra-extra credit, do that with an enemy.

Helpful Resources

Recommended books, periodicals, websites, movies, and music:

Gregory Boyd, *The Myth of a Christian Nation* (Zondervan)

Shane Claiborne, "What Would Jesus Cut? Who Would Jesus Bomb?" (sojo.net/blogs/2011/02/28/what-would-jesus-cut-who-would-jesus-bomb)

Hotel Rwanda film (www.imdb.com/title/tt0395169/)

The National Priorities Project (www.nationalpriorities.org/)

Project on Defense Alternatives (www.comw.org/pda/)

Ronald J. Sider, *Fixing the Moral Deficit: A Balanced Way to Balance the Budget* (InterVarsity Press)

Flannery O'Connor, *A Good Man Is Hard to Find* (Harcourt Brace Jovanovich)

Schindler's List film (www.imdb.com/title/tt0108052/)

The War Resisters League (www.warresisters.org/pages/piechart.htm)

Personal Reflections

Use this space to jot down a prayer or any thoughts and questions this material has sparked. How is God speaking to you?

_____

_____

_____

_____

_____

_____

_____

_____

_____

_____

_____

_____

_____

Conclusion

It's about imagination.

Sometimes the only thing stopping us is our imagination, our ability to envision a world that is different than the one we have now.

The biblical prophets had that kind of imagination, which is why they were such eccentric advocates for justice. Micah and Isaiah speak about a day when we will beat our swords into plows and our spears into pruning hooks ... inviting us to imagine a world where we have turned the things that have brought death into things that bring life. It's a wonderful thought to imagine military Humvees turned into farm tractors.

Anyone who refuses to accept things as they are runs the risk of being called a dreamer, an idealist, or crazy. But there is a great line from an old guy named Peter Maurin[1] who started communities all over the world committed to peacemaking. He said, "If I am crazy ... it is because I refuse to be crazy in the same way that the world has gone crazy."

It's all a matter of perspective. Some might say it is crazy to challenge the current economic patterns where 1 percent of the world controls nearly half the world's stuff, because capitalism is the best system we've ever had. *We* say it is crazy to think that

---

1. To learn more about Peter Maurin, see *Peter Maurin: Apostle to the World*, by Dorothy Day (Orbis, 2004).

the world will ever be safe as long as masses live in poverty so that a handful of folks can live as they wish. Some might say that cutting military spending will make the world more dangerous. *We* say maybe we should share our billions so we don't need to hide behind a defense shield with all our stuff. After all, what was attacked on September 11, 2001 was the symbol of the global economy and the weapons that protect it.

Before every great movement that has changed the world, everyone said it was impossible ... and after every great movement, everyone looked back and said it was inevitable. Faith is about believing despite the evidence ... and watching the evidence change. Robert Kennedy put it like this: "You see things; and you say, 'Why?' But I dream things that never were; and I say, 'Why not?'" *Jesus, Bombs, and Ice Cream* is about reimagining the world.

"This for a world that has lost its imagination."

— doctor in Baghdad, pointing to the bombs as they fell from the sky

Small Group Leader Helps

To ensure a successful small group experience, read the following information before beginning.

Group Preparation

Whether your small group has been meeting together for years or is gathering for the first time, be sure to designate a consistent time and place to work through the six sessions. Once you establish the when and where of your times together, select a facilitator who will keep discussions on track and an eye on the clock. If you choose to rotate this responsibility, assign the six sessions to their respective facilitators upfront, so they can prepare their thoughts and questions prior to the session they are responsible for leading. Follow the same assignment procedure should your group want to serve any snacks (ice cream, anyone?) or beverages.

A Note to Facilitators

As facilitator, you are responsible for honoring the agreed-upon time frame of each meeting, for prompting helpful discussion among your group, and for keeping the dialogue equitable by drawing out quieter members and helping more talkative participants to remember that others' insights are also valued in your group.

You might find it helpful to preview each session's video teaching segment and then scan the "Video Discussion" questions that pertain to it. Before your group meets, ask God to guide the discussion, and then be sensitive to the direction in which he wishes to lead.

Urge participants to bring their study guide, pen, and a Bible to every gathering.

Session Format

Each session of the *Jesus, Bombs, and Ice Cream* study is planned for about an hour, but may be expanded should your group have more time available. Every session of the study guide includes the following group components:

- **Checking In** (sessions 2–6)—an opportunity to briefly revisit the previous session to raise any follow-up questions or insights from the between-session activities

- **Introduction**—an entrée to the session's topic, which may be read by a volunteer or summarized by the facilitator

- **Video Teaching**—an outline of the session's video teaching (which lasts 8–15 minutes) for group members to follow along and take notes if they wish

- **Video Discussion**—video-related and Bible exploration questions that reinforce the session content and elicit personal input from every group member

Additionally, in each session you will find these personal tools:

- **Actions to Consider Between Sessions**—several ideas to help you apply or further investigate the session content

- **Helpful Resources**—recommended books, periodicals, websites, movies, and music that coincide with the session content

- **Personal Reflections**—a journaling page to record how God is speaking to you through the session content

Share Your Thoughts

With the Author: Your comments will be forwarded to the author when you send them to *zauthor@zondervan.com*.

With Zondervan: Submit your review of this book by writing to *zreview@zondervan.com*.

Free Online Resources at
www.zondervan.com

Zondervan AuthorTracker: Be notified whenever your favorite authors publish new books, go on tour, or post an update about what's happening in their lives at www.zondervan.com/authortracker.

Daily Bible Verses and Devotions: Enrich your life with daily Bible verses or devotions that help you start every morning focused on God. Visit www.zondervan.com/newsletters.

Free Email Publications: Sign up for newsletters on Christian living, academic resources, church ministry, fiction, children's resources, and more. Visit www.zondervan.com/newsletters.

Zondervan Bible Search: Find and compare Bible passages in a variety of translations at www.zondervanbiblesearch.com.

Other Benefits: Register yourself to receive online benefits like coupons and special offers, or to participate in research.

ZONDERVAN®

ZONDERVAN.com/
AUTHORTRACKER
follow your favorite authors